FULLY ALIVE

FULLY ALIVE

ACTION GUIDE

A Journey that Will Change Your Life

KEN DAVIS

THOMAS NELSON
Since 1798

NASHVILLE   DALLAS   MEXICO CITY   RIO DE JANEIRO

Published in Nashville, Tennessee, by Thomas Nelson, Inc.

ISBN: 978-1-4016-7528-8

Printed in the United States of America

12 13 14 15 16 QG 5 4 3 2 1

"For to me, to live is Christ, and to die is gain."
—**Paul, in Philippians 1:21 (NIV)**

CONTENTS

HOW TO USE THIS GUIDE

Thank you for choosing to live fully alive! This action guide was designed to accompany the *Fully Alive* DVD. Our hope is that you will use this guide in a group setting such as a Bible study, Sunday school class, or small group gathering to work through each of the seven sessions in order. Each session takes about an hour to complete, and can be completed weekly, bi-weekly, monthly, or whatever works best for your group.

Each group should have a facilitator who is responsible for starting the video session, keeping track of time, and guiding discussion. The facilitator is also the person who may read aloud questions, prompt group members to respond, and ensure that everyone has the opportunity to participate.

For your study each person should have his or her own action guide. Group members are also encouraged to have a copy of the book *Fully Alive* by Ken Davis, although the study can be finished with just the action guide and DVD.

Here's an overview of what each group session will look like:

❯ INTRODUCTION – Prepare for the session individually.

❯ GET STARTED – Read a brief overview of the session's theme.

❯ GET CONNECTED – Respond to a question on the session's theme.

❯ GIVE YOUR HEART AND MIND TO GOD – Ask God for wisdom and direction as you begin the session.

❯ LEARN TOGETHER – View the session chapter on the *Fully Alive* DVD.

❯ DISCUSSION – Talk about ideas and insights ignited by the DVD content.

❯ EXPLORATION – Study a relevant passage of Scripture for more insight about the session's theme.

❯ REFLECTION – Discover how the session can transform your life.

▷ NOW IS THE TIME – Identify personal next steps based upon the session's theme.

▷ CLOSE WITH PRAYER – Finish your group time with prayer.

During your group time you may find that you are not always able to get through all of the questions for each session. That's okay! Remember, the point is not to get through all of the questions. The point is for your group to open up and ask God to speak to you about how you can start living fully alive.

Are you ready to begin? All you need is your group, a TV or computer with DVD capability, a Bible, a pen or pencil, and this action guide. To learn more about living fully alive, and Ken Davis, visit Kendavis.com. There you will find Ken's blog, upcoming events, other resources, and ways to connect.

We are excited that by participating in this study you are taking a next step in order to live fully alive for God's glory. May God bless you on your journey!

FULLY ALIVE

Introduction

When was the last time you felt the rush of excitement as you raced down a hill on your bike? When was the last morning you leapt out of bed, excited about the opportunities the day would bring? When was the last time you felt the power of Christ as you used your talents to live for his glory? When was the last time you felt that you were living fully alive? Has it been awhile?

The reality is that many of us have allowed the busyness of life to prevent us from living our lives fully alive. Instead of living lives of action, we have chosen to live lives of reaction, and we are missing out. Let's change that . . . it's time to live fully alive!

Get Started — 1 minute

Have someone in the group read aloud this brief description of the session theme.

Welcome! As you begin your *Fully Alive* study together, be prepared to see God do amazing things in the lives of your group members. With this in mind, it is important that each person commits to fully participating in each session.

In this opening session you are invited to explore what it means to live life fully alive. You are invited to stop living with your eyes *half closed*, and start living with your eyes *wide open*.

> *"The glory of God is man fully alive."*
> —*St. Irenaeus*

Get Connected — 3 minutes

Share your response to the following question:

What is the first image that comes to mind when you hear the expression "fully alive"?

Give Your Heart and Mind to God — 1 minute

Making a decision to live fully alive may cause you to look at your life in new ways. It may cause you to confront your fears, wrestle with regrets, and ask new questions. As you prepare your heart and mind for session one, open in prayer, asking God for the courage. Ask God to awaken a passion in your life that knows no bounds.

Learn Together — 13 minutes

If you'd like to take a few notes as you watch the session one video segment, use the space below.

Discussion: "Fully Alive" — 12 minutes

You may not have time to discuss all of the questions in this section—that's okay! Cover as many as you can, encouraging everyone to participate.

1. As you listened to Ken Davis speak about living fully alive, what words, phrases, or ideas stuck out to you?

2. When have you felt you were merely trudging through the paces of life?

3. What would you need to change in your life in order to live fully alive?

4. Ken Davis has written that the impulse to live fully alive is "so strong that people spend billions of dollars every year on drugs and diets and creams that claim to bring new life . . . what people don't often realize is that the passion for living is a God thing." How have you tried in the past to live fully alive?

Exploration — 12 minutes

Read Philippians 3:10–14 and discuss your answers to the following questions:

1. Do you believe the power of the resurrection is available to followers of Jesus now?

2. Where have you seen it?

3. What does it mean to "lay hold of that for which Christ Jesus has also laid hold of me"?

4. How can we reach out and lay hold of the life God means for us to live?

Reflection — 12 minutes

During this section it is time to look inside and discover how this session can transform your life.

In order to define a path for living fully alive Ken challenges us to look back at our lives for the moments where God has driven a stake in the ground. Ken says, "Look at those moments where you felt fully alive and you might discover a secret as to what you'll have to put in your life to be what God created you to be."

Take a few moments to write down some of the stakes in the ground from your past, those moments of personal revelation, and then answer the following questions as a group.

Give everyone in your group a chance to respond.

1. What is one key stake you have discovered in your life?

2. Was it hard to identify stakes in your life? Why?

3. When you look back and see the stakes in your life lined up, how do you see those stakes leading you in a new direction toward living fully alive today?

Ken Davis also shared that stakes in the ground are not only things God has placed in our past, but also things we can put ahead of us. Considering the following areas, take a few moments to write down stakes you would like to put ahead of you in order to become fully alive, and then answer the following questions.

Physically

Spiritually

Mentally

Socially

1. What is one stake you are putting in the ground to become fully alive?

2. What is one way you need help putting your stakes in the ground?

3. How can you as a group work together to help each other put stakes in the ground?

Now is the Time — 5 minutes

Henry David Thoreau is credited with saying, "Most men lead lives of quiet desperation and go to the grave with the song still in them."

We all wake up in the morning with opportunities before us and choices to make. We can either follow our dreams, and sing the song God has given us, or continue to live each day just like the day before and go to the grave with our song still in us.

As you close this session, take a moment to discuss together what it means for you to live your life fully alive, answering the following question:

"What song is God asking me to sing with my life?"

Close with Prayer — 1 Minute

The end of this time together is really the beginning of the opportunity for you and your group to live fully alive. It is essential for each member of the group to commit to look deep within and to be willing to openly share with one another.

Take a moment and offer a prayer of thanksgiving and commitment to God, such as the one that follows:

Dear heavenly Father, as a group of people who love you and want to be found in faithful obedience to what you've called us to do, we ask . . .

What do you want us to learn while we're on this journey toward becoming fully alive? What stakes in the ground have you placed in our lives so far? What new stakes in the ground can we place today? We want to know the power of the resurrection in our lives. We want to glorify you as we live fully alive. Amen.

OBSTACLES AND OPPORTUNITIES

Introduction

There is a thrill that occurs when you start to live fully alive. Like putting on a pair of glasses for the first time, you experience a moment of clarity as the blurry images of past mistakes and a lack of direction are transformed into clear pictures of wisdom and purpose. Yet this thrill does not always last.

Frankly, the second you decide to live fully alive you will begin to notice that in the midst of glorious opportunities there are all kinds of obstacles. These obstacles will threaten to derail and squelch your newfound passion for life. They will attempt to extinguish the fire of life that you feel burning inside you.

But wait! There is good news! Are you ready to hear it?

Get Started — 1 minute

Have someone in the group read aloud this brief description of the session theme.

In this session you will not only discover how to name the obstacles that are holding you back from living fully alive, but how to *overcome* them. And in the end you will discover the hope that Christ has for you as you live each day fully alive.

> "Anything worth doing is worth doing badly." *
> —G.K. Chesterton

---

* G. K. Chesterton, "When Doctors Agree," *Paradoxes of Mr Pond* (Kelly Bray, Cornwall, UK: House of Stratus, 2008), 41.

Get Connected — 3 minutes

In less than ten words, answer the following question:

What obstacles may be keeping you from living fully alive?

Give Your Heart and Mind to God — 1 minute

Now it is time to prepare your heart and mind for session two. Take a few minutes to pray together for your group meeting. Ask God to help you overcome the obstacles in your life, recognize the blessings he has for you, and help you move forward in living fully alive.

Learn Together — 16 minutes

If you'd like to take a few notes as you watch the session two video segment, use the space below.

Discussion: "Obstacles and Opportunities" — 10 minutes

You may not have time to discuss all of the questions in this section—that's okay! Cover as many as you can, encouraging everyone to participate.

1. As you listened to Ken share about the obstacles that he has faced in living fully alive, what words, phrases, or ideas stuck out to you?

2. Ken mentioned fear and perfectionism as two of the obstacles he has faced in life; what obstacles have you faced?

3. When have you had the opportunity to see a "Nooooooo!" picture of yourself, a picture that allowed you to see yourself from a new perspective?

4. Were you pleased with what you saw?

5. Did you see a blessing in your "No!" picture?

6. How did you respond?

Exploration — 12 minutes

Read Matthew 26:33–35, 73–75 and discuss your answers to the following questions:

1. How confident was Peter in his loyalty to Jesus and in his courage to face difficult challenges?

2. What was Peter's reaction to the prophetic statement in 26:34 by Jesus about him?

3. Before this incident, do you think Peter felt that he
   was one of the more trusted disciples of Jesus?

4. How surprised was Peter by his behavior in the face
   of opposition?

*Read 1 Peter 1:6–7 and discuss your answers to the fol-
lowing questions:*

1. This statement by Peter was written over thirty years
   after the death of Jesus. Do you think Peter learned
   much through his denial of Jesus?

2. Do you think this should be considered a "stake in the
   ground" moment for Peter?

3. How had Peter's attitude changed in the thirty years?

Reflection — 12 minutes

During this section it is time to look inside and discover how this session can transform your life.

A key takeaway from the life of Peter is that while he could have been depressed and ashamed in the face of his behavioral failure, he instead chose to take advantage of the failures and opportunities he had by using the mercy God had shown him. And as we work to overcome the obstacles in our own lives, we can do the same.

Specifically, Ken spoke of three ways you can overcome the obstacles in your life and take advantage of the opportunities that God is giving you. Let's take some time to work through each.

LOOK AT THE PICTURE

First, using the space below, write down words in order to create a picture of your life right now. For example, you could write down the different roles you have, the obstacles you've identified, your spiritual gifts, the things you are passionate about, your abilities, personality traits that describe you, positive and negative experiences from your life, and your unique talents.

RECOGNIZE THE BLESSING

Second, now that you have a clear picture of your life, use the space below to write any blessings and opportunities you see in front of you. What opportunities might God be asking you to pursue?

MOVE FORWARD

Finally, write down the very next step you need to take in order to pursue what God is calling you to do. As a group, you should also make a commitment to help each other in taking the steps you identify.

Now is the Time — 5 minutes

As you finish this session, remember the words of the apostle Paul in Philippians 4:8:

> "Whatever is true, whatever is noble, whatever is right, whatever is pure, whatever is lovely, whatever is admirable – if anything is excellent or praiseworthy – think about such things." (NIV)

Be encouraged to stay positive as you work with your group to overcome the obstacles in your life and go after the opportunities God is giving you. Remember, just as Ken said, "God isn't looking for perfection, he is looking for obedience."

The reality is that you will fall; it will hurt, but in the end it will be worth it. Make sure to pace yourself, let God lead you along the way, and never give up. Live fully alive!

Close with Prayer — 1 minute

The end of this time together is really the beginning of the opportunity for you and your group to remove obstacles and seize opportunities in your lives. It is essential for each member of the group to commit to look deep within and to be willing to openly share with one another.

Take a moment to offer a prayer of thanksgiving and commitment to God, such as the one that follows:

Dear heavenly Father, today we are making a decision to lean on the hope that Christ offers us, and to move forward knowing that you work together all things for good for those who love you and are called according to your purposes. We make a decision as a group to trust one another, and to help each other overcome the obstacles in our lives. We see clearly that you have given us great opportunities to live fully alive, and today we plant a stake in the ground to go after them. May the power of your Spirit guide us, and may we do all things for your glory alone. Amen.

GOALS

Introduction

Isn't it amazing that, out of the billions of people in the world, God did not make any two people the same? Beyond just our physical differences, some of the most amazing differences we have are the gifts God has given each person. One person is a gifted public speaker, and another person is a gifted writer. One person is a talented chef, and another person is a talented mechanic.

When you start to understand this you will see that because of your God-given, unique giftedness, you have a clear reason to make a difference in the world. As a result, you will see that it is important for you to make goals that will allow you to use your gifts for God's glory.

Get Started — 1 minute

Have someone in the group read aloud this brief description of the session theme:

Take a moment to look at the other people in your group. Isn't it pretty clear that you are different from the person sitting next to you? In this session you will not only discover the unique gifts God has given you, but you will also learn how to make goals that give you a chance to use them. In doing so you will learn to live life fully alive!

> *"How do you eat an elephant? One bite at a time."*
> **—Unknown**

Get Connected — 3 minutes

In one or two sentences, answer the following question:

What is one goal you have set for yourself in the past?

Become more involved in church.

Give Your Heart and Mind to God — 1 minute

Now it is time to prepare your heart and mind for session three. Take a few minutes to pray together for your group meeting. Ask God to give you wisdom as you reflect upon who you have been in the past, who you are today, and who you would like to be in the future. Ask God to help you make clear goals and to take the steps necessary to achieve them.

Learn Together — 20 minutes

If you'd like to take a few notes as you watch the session three video segment, use the space below.

Discussion: "Goals" — 10 minutes

You may not have time to discuss all of the questions in this section—that's okay! Cover as many as you can, encouraging everyone to participate.

1. What is one of the gifts you believe God has given you?

2. Do you see any gifts in other group members that they might not be aware of?

3. Share with the group a time when you felt like you were able to use your gifts in order to achieve a goal of great value. What made it valuable?

4. Are you currently involved in any situations where you feel that you are not able to use your gifts?

5. What is one goal you would like to use your God-given gifts to achieve?

Exploration — 10 minutes

Read Nehemiah 2:11–20 and discuss your answers to the following questions:

1. How did he use his gifts for God's glory?

2. What is one example of how Nehemiah showed that he had a sense of purpose in achieving his goals?

3. How did Nehemiah maintain a positive attitude when opposition arose?

4. What was Nehemiah's reaction to ridicule and threat?

5. What do you do in the face of opposition?

Reflection — 12 minutes

During this section it is time to look inside and discover how this session can transform your life.

Are you ready to use your giftedness to achieve goals for God's glory and live fully alive? Use the following exercise to help you get started.

1. In each of the areas listed below, write down the goal that will give you the greatest sense of accomplishment.

2. Within each area, write down one or two milestones that will lead to the accomplishment of each goal.

3. Now rank each of your four goals according to how important they are for you to achieve.

4. For the top-ranked goal write down the absolute next step you need to take in order to achieve your goal.

5. Take a few minutes to share your top-ranked goal with the rest of the group.

Physical

Social

Mental

Spiritual

"Test me, O LORD . . . examine my heart and my mind."
Psalm 26:2 (NIV)

Now is the Time — 5 minutes

"Life doesn't have a winner's circle; it has a finish line."
—Ken Davis

The truth is that there is a finish line at the end of our lives, and this gives us a choice as to how we live now. We can choose to saunter our way toward that finish line, never giving everything we have to use our gifts for God's glory; or we can run hard, exhausting every opportunity. Choose to run hard.

The great news is that you don't have to run the race alone. There are people around you who can help you make it, and the Bible is filled with examples of people who have lived their lives making the most of every opportunity.

As a group, commit to read the following verse each day before your next session. It is a verse that will inspire you as you follow through on achieving the goals you have chosen. You may find it helpful to memorize this verse:

> "Therefore we also, since we are surrounded by so great a cloud of witnesses, let us lay aside every weight, and the sin which so easily ensnares us, and let us run with endurance the race that is set before us." (Hebrews 12:1, NKJV)

Remember, things that don't change are dead.

Decide to be different.

Decide to make changes.

Decide to use your gifts.

Decide to set goals.

Decide to live fully alive.

Close with Prayer — 1 minute

The end of this time together is really the beginning of the opportunity for you and your group to remove obstacles and seize opportunities in your lives. It is essential for each member of the group to commit to look deep within and to be willing to openly share with one another.

Take a moment to offer a prayer of thanksgiving and commitment to God, such as the one that follows:

Dear heavenly Father, today we have made a decision to stop dreaming about what you want us to be. Instead, we have decided to start doing something that will make us different tomorrow. We have decided to run with endurance the race you have set before us. We have decided to set goals that allow us to use our gifts for your glory. As we face the obstacles that will come our way, remind us that living fully alive is about being everything you have created us to be. Amen.

NOT ALONE

Introduction

Have you made the decision to live fully alive? If you've made it this far in the study, hopefully the answer is yes. In fact, at this point in your study . . .

Your heart should be pounding in response to the words of St. Irenaeus: "The glory of God is man fully alive." You should be moving forward and doing the hard work of seizing the opportunities hiding among the obstacles in your life. You should be setting goals that give you the opportunity to use your giftedness for God's glory. You should be doing all of these things . . . and all of these things are great!

But . . .

You must understand that if you're trying to do all of these things alone . . . by yourself . . . you're going to fail.

Get Started — 1 minute

Have someone in the group read aloud this brief description of the session theme.

Throughout our lives we have the opportunity to experience different kinds of friendships. From playing outside with the friends of our childhood neighborhood, to the lifelong friendship of a spouse, friendships are a significant part of our lives. In this session you will learn how to understand what real friendships are, how to make friendships that really matter, and how these friendships can help you live fully alive.

> *"The next best thing to being wise oneself is to live in a circle of those who are."*
> —C. S. Lewis

Get Connected — 3 minutes

In less than three sentences, answer the following question:

Who was your closest friend as a child? Describe that person.

Give Your Heart and Mind to God — 1 minute

Now it is time to prepare your heart and mind for session four. Take a few minutes to pray together for your group meeting. Ask God to give you a desire to have intimate friendships and a clear understanding of the steps you need to take to do so. Ask God to help you understand the different categories of friendships and how the love of Christ can be the foundation of all of your friendships.

Learn Together — 16 minutes

If you'd like to take a few notes as you watch the session four video segment, use the space below.

Discussion: "Not Alone" — 10 minutes

You may not have time to discuss all of the questions in this section—that's okay! Cover as many as you can, encouraging everyone to participate.

1. Why does it seem that some people have many friends while others don't seem to have any?

2. Is it possible that people with many friends are as lonely as people without friends?

3. Either tell of a time when you knew someone was your best friend, or tell of a time when someone you thought was a close friend turned out to not feel that way about you.

4. What was it about your friendship that was different than other friendships? Or how did it feel when you realized that they did not want to be as close to you as you did to them?

Exploration — 12 minutes

Read Acts 9:26–30; 11:22–26 and discuss your answers to the following questions:

1. How did Barnabas respond to Paul's conversion differently than the other believers?

2. How important do you think the friendship of Barnabas was to the future ministry of Paul?

3. What chief character traits of Barnabas are revealed in this passage?

4. How do you think Paul would have described Barnabas?

Reflection — 12 minutes

During this section it is time to look inside and discover how this session can transform your life.

"You might be able to survive without friends, but you cannot live fully alive."
—Ken Davis

Once you realize that in order to live fully alive you must have close friendships, it is important to understand that there are different categories of friendships. Bill Gothard, founder of the Institute in Basic Life Principles, categorized friendships on four levels:

> An **acquaintance** is a person you're in contact with rarely or only once, such as someone you meet while traveling or who comes to your house to fix the plumbing or washing machine.

> A **casual friendship** is based on common interests or activities. A casual friend may be a person at work or someone you know at a club, at church, or on a sports team.

▷ A **close friendship** is based on mutual life goals and long-term interests. The two of you are beginning to see potential achievement in each other's lives. You discuss specific goals and assume a personal responsibility for developing them. These friends can make suggestions about important aspects of your life.

▷ An **intimate friendship** is based on open honesty, discretion, and a commitment to the development of each other's character and spiritual potential. You will help each other through trials and sorrows. You will assume personal responsibility for each other's reputations. You are sensitive to traits and attitudes that you both need to improve. Intimate friends are committed to faithfulness, loyalty, and availability.*

Our lives are best lived when we are developing friendships in each of these categories. In the space below, write down at least one friend you have in each category.

---

* Bill Gothard, *Institute in Basic Life Principles* (Oak Brook, IL: IBLP, 1989), 167.

Friendship Categories	Friends in Each Category
ACQUAINTANCE	
CASUAL FRIEND	
CLOSE FRIEND	
INTIMATE FRIEND	

Now is the Time — 5 minutes

Now that you understand the categories of friendships you need in life, it is important to know how to make new friendships. According to Ken, the answer is fairly straightforward:

In order to make new friendships you must be the kind of friend you are looking for to someone else.

Yes, you are going to have to take risks. And yes, when you choose to risk your heart with friends, you will fall; it will hurt, but it will be worth it!

At its core, the concept of friendship and love comes from Jesus, who said, "A new command I give you: Love one another. As I have loved you, so you must love one another" (John 13:34, NIV).

The love Jesus showed was grounded in sacrifice. Jesus gave his life for others. In order for you to experience intimate friendships, you must do the same. You must humbly take the risk to get to know someone else.

As you close this session make a decision to take one risk in an effort to build a deeper friendship with someone else. Use the space below to write that person's name and what risk you are going to take.

Close with Prayer — 1 minute

The end of this time together is really the beginning of the opportunity for you and your group to develop deep friendships in your lives. It is essential for each member of the group to commit to look deep within and to be willing to openly share with one another.

Take a moment to offer a prayer of thanksgiving and commitment to God, such as the one that follows:

Dear heavenly Father, we thank you for the love you have displayed in sending your son Jesus to show us what it means to love others. Today we commit to show others that same kind of love. Please help us to build intimate friendships. Please help us to live fully alive. Amen.

BAGGAGE

Guilt and Forgiveness

Introduction

As you begin this session, take a moment to consider the apostle Paul. Once a legalistic, hypocritical Pharisee named Saul, Paul's life was transformed when he encountered Jesus on the road to Damascus.

After his encounter, Paul could've easily buried himself under the burdens of guilt, sin, and bitterness caused by remembering his past. Instead he found forgiveness and freedom in letting his burdens go. He became single-minded in purpose, and God used him in amazing ways for his glory.

Perhaps you find yourself living under heavy burdens weighing down your life. Does it seem unbearable? Are there memories you can't seem to erase? Are there decisions you've made that you wish you could change? Perhaps it is time for you to find the same forgiveness and freedom Paul found. Perhaps it is time to drop your baggage and live fully alive.

Get Started — 1 minute

Have someone in the group read aloud this brief description of the session theme.

Life is a long journey, and if you want to get the most out of it you must live without the burden of anything that will hinder you from crossing the finish line. In this session you will learn to identify the baggage in life that you are holding on to. Once you have done that you will learn how to take the steps necessary to drop your baggage once and for all. You will learn to run full speed ahead, living fully alive.

> *"Whether you think you can or can't, you're right."* *
> **—Henry Ford**

Get Connected — 3 minutes

In a few words, answer the following question:

What does it mean to be free in Christ?

---

* Quoted in Bob Lodie, "It's All About Beliefs," *The Small Business Brief*, newsletter, http://www.small businessbrief.com/articles/inspiration/003753.html#top.

Give Your Heart and Mind to God — I minute

Now it is time to prepare your heart and mind for session five. Take a few minutes to pray together for your group meeting. Ask God to help you identify the baggage you are holding on to that is preventing you from living fully alive. Ask God to help you let go of that baggage so that you can know Christ more fully, with the power of his resurrection burning inside you.

Learn Together — 17 minutes

If you'd like to take a few notes as you watch the session five video segment, use the space below.

Discussion: "Baggage: Guilt and Forgiveness" — 10 minutes

You may not have time to discuss all of the questions in this section—that's okay! Cover as many as you can, encouraging everyone to participate.

1. How does guilt stop you from living?

2. What are the things that you keep coming back to that discourage you or cause you to feel guilt and shame?

3. Are there things you're feeling guilty about that you don't need to feel guilty about?

4. How will ridding your life of "stuff" help you be all that God wants you to be?

5. Go a step further as a group in being open and honest with each other. Is there any "stuff" in other group members' lives that you feel they might not be able to see themselves?

Exploration — 12 minutes

Read Acts 7:59–8:3 and discuss your answers to the following questions:

1. How did Saul, also known as the apostle Paul, participate in Stephen's stoning?

2. How might this event have affected Paul once he became a follower of Jesus?

Read Galatians 1:13–14; 2:6–10 and discuss your answers to the following questions:

1. How did Paul understand his Jewish heritage and his zealous opposition to the gospel?

2. How did others understand Paul's background as a Pharisee?

3. How did Paul use his baggage of legalism and extreme Judaism to the advantage of the Galatians?

Reflection ⸱⸱⸱ 12 ⸱ minutes

During this section it is time to look inside and discover how this session can transform your life.

It is important that you now take time to make sense of the baggage in your life. It is one thing to talk about what is holding you back, but now it is important for you to take some time to write it down. Doing so will allow you to throw off everything that hinders you and get rid of the things that are preventing you from living fully alive.

Use the space below to write down areas of your life where you feel guilt. Write down recurring problems that you struggle with. Be sure to write down things from your past, but also current expectations and realities that may be causing you to feel guilt. Be honest with yourself. If something is too hard to write down, perhaps you could write down a letter to represent it.

Finally, use the space below to write down some of the "stuff" that you feel you need to get rid of. This could be physical "stuff," time commitments, hobbies, or habits that are slowing you down.

As the group is comfortable, share at least one thing each person wrote down.

Now is the Time — 5 minutes

Here is some good news! You can take everything you wrote above and lay it down at the foot of the cross, a place where you will find forgiveness . . . a clean slate.

Jesus took all of your burdens to the cross, and if you trust in him as your Lord and Savior you are forgiven. God can take your life and use it for his glory, and you can echo the words of the apostle Paul when he says, "I press on to take hold of that for which Christ Jesus took hold of me" (Philippians 3:12, NIV).

God can use everything that's happened to you in order to help you live fully alive today.

Close with Prayer — 1 minute

The end of this time together is really the beginning of the opportunity for you and your group to drop your burdens and live fully alive. It is essential for each member of the group to commit to look deep within and to be willing to openly share with one another.

Take a moment to offer a prayer of thanksgiving and commitment to God, such as the one that follows:

Dear heavenly Father, thank you for your grace and forgiveness. Today we drop all of our burdens at the foot of the cross of your son Jesus. Today we find true freedom. Help us to live fully alive. Amen.

FAITH AND RISK

Introduction

Were you a risk taker when you were a child? Did you find ways to do things others might consider harmful or dangerous because they gave you the chance to do something amazing and incredible? Now that you are older, and "wiser," do you still take these types of risks?

Unfortunately, your answer is probably "No." It seems that the older we get the fewer risks we're willing to take; and as the days go by, many of us choose to be fearful instead of daring. Yet the reality is that a person who is living fully alive is a risk taker. They have decided to let go of what is secure and discover that God can be trusted. They are risk takers for God.

Get Started — 1 minute

Have someone in the group read aloud this brief description of the session theme.

In this session you will learn how to be a risk taker every day of your life . . . if not every second. You will have the opportunity to move from a position of fear to a position of confident faith. Remember, whenever the risk is part of living fully alive—to glorify God—it's a risk worth taking!

> *"For to me, to live is Christ, and to die is gain."*
> —*Paul, in Philippians 1:21 (NIV)*

Get Connected — 3 minutes

In one or two sentences, answer the following question:

What is the biggest risk you've ever taken?

Give Your Heart and Mind to God — 1 minute

Now it is time to prepare your heart and mind for session six. Take a few minutes to pray together for your group meeting. Ask God to help you unmask your biggest fears so that you can overcome them. Ask God to renew a childlike passion to be a risk taker for his glory.

Learn Together — 12 minutes ////////////////////////

If you'd like to take a few notes as you watch the session six video segment, use the space below.

Discussion: "Faith and Risk" — 12 minutes ///////////

You may not have time to discuss all of the questions in this section—that's okay! Cover as many as you can, encouraging everyone to participate.

1. Can you remember a time when you took an obvious risk without knowing whether or not you would succeed?

2. Can you remember a time when you failed to take a risk and you wished you had stepped out in faith instead?

3. Describe one person you know whom you would call a risk taker. What is it about their life that causes you to believe that?

4. How important is it for followers of Jesus to be risk takers?

5. If we are not to fear taking risks for God, what does it say about people who seem to be constantly afraid?

6. What can fear say about a person's view of God?

7. What kind of risk taker do you want to become?

Exploration — 12 minutes

Read Exodus 3:11–15; 4:11–17 and discuss your answers to the following questions:

1. According to the passage, what risks did God ask Moses to take?

2. How did Moses respond to what God asked him to do?

3. What were some of the reasons Moses gave explaining how he couldn't do what God was asking him to do?

4. How did God respond?

5. How might God respond to our fears?

Reflection — 12 minutes

During this section it is time to look inside and discover how this session can transform your life.

Fear can be disabling. Even when we know that God is asking us to take a risk, fear has the power to extinguish our ability to do what he asks us to do. In an effort to banish fear from your life, please take time to do the following exercise, using page 79.

1. Write the word "fear" in tiny, lowercase letters at the bottom of the page.

2. At the top of the page write the word "CONFI-DENCE" in bold, uppercase letters.

3. Go back to the bottom of the page and just above the word "fear," write down all of the things you are afraid of in tiny, lowercase letters.

4. Finally, copy the keys from the 23rd Psalm that bring you hope and confidence beneath the word "CON-FIDENCE." Write boldly.

> [1]The LORD is my shepherd;
> I shall not want.
> [2]He makes me to lie down in green pastures;
> He leads me beside the still waters.
> [3]He restores my soul;
> He leads me in the paths of righteousness
> For His name's sake.

⁴Yea, though I walk through the valley of the
shadow of death,
I will fear no evil;
For You are with me;
Your rod and Your staff, they comfort me.
⁵You prepare a table before me in the presence of
my enemies;
You anoint my head with oil;
My cup runs over.
⁶Surely goodness and mercy shall follow me
All the days of my life;
And I will dwell in the house of the LORD
Forever.

Psalm 23 (NKJV)

Answer the following questions as a group:

1. How did it feel to write out all of the things that you are afraid of?

2. How do the words of Psalm 23 affect how you feel about your fears?

Now is the Time — 5 minutes

Ken Davis has written, "Almost every worthy goal I have ever dared to commit to writing down has become a reality." Until your next meeting, make a commitment to record daily your highs and lows, your goals, your successes and failures, and the opportunities you had to take risks for God's glory. As you write, ask yourself, "What risk is God asking me to take?" Is it sharing Christ with a friend? Is it taking steps to heal a relationship? Is it apologizing to someone you've hurt? In each situation, be ready to start taking risks for God.

Close with Prayer — 1 minute

The end of this time together is really the beginning of the opportunity for you and your group to face your fears and determine to take risks for God. It is essential for each member of the group to commit to look deep within and to be willing to openly share with one another.

Take a moment to offer a prayer of thanksgiving and commitment to God, such as the one that follows:

> [1]The Eternal is my shepherd, He cares for me
> always.
> [2]He provides me rest in rich, green fields
> beside streams of refreshing water.
> *He soothes my fears;*
> [3]He makes me whole again,
> steering me *off worn, hard paths*
> to roads where *truth and* righteousness echo
> His name.
> [4]Even in the *unending* shadows of death's
> darkness,
> I am not overcome by fear.

Because You are with me *in those dark moments,*
    near with Your protection and guidance,
        I am comforted.
⁵You spread out a table before me,
    provisions in the midst of *attack from* my
        enemies;
You *care for all my needs,* anointing my head with
    soothing, fragrant oil,
        filling my cup again and again *with Your*
        grace.
⁶Certainly Your faithful protection and loving
    provision will pursue me
    where I go, always, everywhere.
I will always be with the Eternal, in Your house
    forever.
    AMEN.

Psalm 23 (THE VOICE)

FINISHING WELL

Introduction

Congratulations! You have made it to the final session of the *Fully Alive* study. Hopefully over the last several weeks you have discovered a passion to live fully alive, and you are now running the race God has set before you.

Over the past weeks you have learned many things. You learned how to look back at your life for the key moments when God has driven a stake in the ground, helping you to understand who God created you to be. You then learned how to set stakes ahead of you that will help you live fully alive.

You learned how to name obstacles in your life that are holding you back, how to find blessings within your obstacles, and how to move forward keeping your eyes on Jesus.

You learned that God has given you unique gifts to use for his glory and how to set goals that will allow you to use your giftedness. You then were challenged to run with endurance the race that God has set before you.

You learned that it is not possible for you to live fully alive by yourself. You must learn to cultivate friendships, and the place to start is by being the kind of friend you are looking for to someone else.

You learned the importance of identifying baggage that you are holding on to and of making the decision to lay it down at the foot of the cross. In the end, God can use everything that's happened to you in order to help you live fully alive for his glory.

You learned to take risks for God's glory and to move from a position of fear to a position of confident faith. You also learned the importance of keeping a journal and were challenged to use a journal to track your progress in living fully alive.

Get Started — 1 minute

Have someone in the group read aloud this brief description of the session theme.

Many times in life we will experience flashes of motivation, like this study, to live fully alive. But all too often when we go back to the business of life we find ourselves falling into the same rut as we were in before. It's time to stop that practice!

In this session you will learn what it means to finish well, to avoid the danger of normalcy, and to embrace the joy of living the rest of your life fully alive!

Get Connected — 3 minutes

In one or two sentences, answer the following question:

What is one way God has used this lesson to help you live fully alive?

Give Your Heart and Mind to God — 1 minute

Now it is time to prepare your heart and mind for session seven. Take a few minutes to pray together for your group meeting. Ask God to help you learn how to finish well. Ask him to help you see how you can take the lessons learned during this series to continue living fully alive.

Learn Together — 12 minutes

If you'd like to take a few notes as you watch the session seven video segment, use the space below.

Discussion: "Finishing Well" — 12 minutes

You may not have time to discuss all of the questions in this section—that's okay! Cover as many as you can, encouraging everyone to participate.

1. How has your life changed over the last six weeks?

2. Looking back at yourself before you started your study, rate yourself on a scale of one to ten with one being "completely out of breath," and ten being "fully alive." Where are you now?

3. What will keep you going once this session is over?

4. What changes have you seen in each other through the course of your study?

5. What are the next steps you are taking to live fully alive?

Exploration — 12 minutes

Read 1 Kings 18:38—19:18 and discuss your answers to the following questions:

1. How did the people respond to the miracle they saw on Mount Carmel?

2. According to Chapter 19, verses 3–5, how did Elijah respond to Jezebel's threat?

3. After experiencing a miracle on Mount Carmel, Elijah is then turned into a fearful runaway at the first word of Jezebel's opposition. Elijah appears to be disoriented and afraid. Where do you see yourself in this story?

4. How does God respond to Elijah when he is found under a bush in the wilderness praying for God to take his life?

5. What is God demonstrating to Elijah?

6. Is Elijah truly alone?

7. What things might God have in store for you if you will trust him enough to risk following him?

Reflection — 12 minutes

During this section it is time to look inside and discover how this session can transform your life.

One way you can begin to avoid living in fear and procrastination is to use the lessons you have learned in this study to create a game plan for living fully alive. The questions below will help you get started.

1. What is one moment in your life where God drove a stake in the ground, and what is one new stake you have driven in the ground?

2. What is one obstacle you have had to overcome in life? What was the opportunity within that obstacle that God is now using?

3. What is one gift that God has given you? What is one goal you have made to use that gift for God's glory?

4. Who is one person with whom you are trying to cultivate a friendship? What step are you taking this week to make that happen?

5. What is one piece of baggage you struggle with holding onto? Have you given it to God? How does it feel to let it go?

6. What is one risk you are taking for God this week?

Now is the Time — 5 minutes

As you move forward in working your game plan, there is one word that will help you. Ken Davis calls it the "D" word:

DISCIPLINE

Discipline is being able to get yourself to take action no matter how you feel about it.

Imagine what you could accomplish if you could get yourself to follow through on your best intentions. Imagine how fully alive your life would be! Imagine how much you could do for God's glory!

Here's the secret . . . discipline is like a muscle. The more you train it, the stronger you will become. The less you train it, the weaker you will become. The question is . . . do you want to be weak or strong?

One way you can help each other to be disciplined is to work together. As you finish this session, take some time to discuss how you can provide accountability for each other as you live fully alive.

Choose someone from within this group or maybe someone outside the group that you feel would be interested in working with you so that you both can become fully alive. What's the name of that person? Set a goal to arrange a meeting so that the two of you can move forward.

And as you move forward, remember . . .

The power of the resurrection is available to you!

The glory of God is man fully alive!

Live! For God's sake . . . LIVE!

Close with Prayer — 1 minute

The end of this time together is really the beginning of the opportunity for you and your group to move forward in living fully alive. It is essential for each member of the group to commit to look deep within and to be willing to openly share with one another.

Take a moment to offer a prayer of thanksgiving and commitment to God, such as the one that follows:

Dear heavenly Father, we desire to know Christ, and the power of his resurrection!

We will run hard, take risks, make goals, and let go of the things that keep us from moving forward. We commit to doing this together. May this study be a stake that you have driven in the ground of our lives. May it change us forever! Help us live fully alive for your glory! Amen.

NOTES

ABOUT THE AUTHOR

Ken Davis, best-selling author and frequent radio and television guest, is a sought-after speaker. His mixture of side-splitting humor and inspiration delights and enriches audiences of all ages.

Ken has been keynote speaker for hundreds of church and major corporate events, and he has made thousands of personal appearances around the world. As president of Dynamic Communications International, he teaches speaking skills to ministry professionals and corporate executives. Ken's daily radio show *Lighten Up!* is heard on more than 1,500 stations in the United States and around the world.

Ken is a graduate of Oak Hills Christian College. He and his wife, Diane, live in Tennessee and have two daughters and six grandchildren. The entire family is involved in Ken's ministry, bringing much laughter and liberating truth to people all across the globe.

Stay connected with Ken!

www.kendavis.com
Twitter: @kendavislive
Facebook: www.facebook.com/kendavis.comedy

Ken Davis Productions
P.O. Box 681568
Franklin, TN 37068
615-599-8955

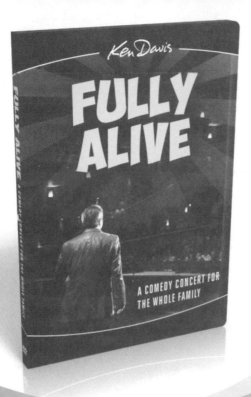

THE NEXT TIME YOU TAKE STAGE, WILL PEOPLE LISTEN?

BECOME A DYNAMIC COMMUNICATOR IN 4 DAYS

Attend our one-of-a-kind, world-class workshop and become the speaker you've always dreamed of.

At the SCORRE conference, you'll go beyond the basics and drill down to the foundations of effective communication. You'll learn to:

- Speak with confidence in any setting
- Deliver crystal clear talks to a captive audience
- Leave your listeners amazed and asking for more

SIGN UP TODAY AT
SCORRECONFERENCE.COM

SCORRE
CONFERENCE

Professional Communicators Summit

The Summit Conference is all about helping speakers, entertainers, entrepreneurs and more turn their skills into a thriving business. After decades in the industry and more than 30 years training speakers as communicators, we know it isn't easy. The Summit Conference was developed to give you a road map to follow and take your career to the top.

AS A SUMMIT PARTICIPANT, YOU WILL LEARN HOW TO:
- Identify your assets and develop your brand.
- Turn your message into potential products.
- Develop a speaking page and media kit event planners will love.
- Build an infrastructure that can sustain the growth you desire.
- Determine your price and make a living doing what you love.

This investment in your career is small compared to the return you'll receive. Give the Summit a shot. We think it just might be the beginning of your dream come true.

REGISTER FOR THE SUMMIT CONFERENCE TODAY!

WWW.COMMUNICATORSSUMMIT.COM